ALIENS
AND UFOS

By John Hawkins

PowerKiDS
press.

New York

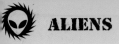

Published in 2012 by The Rosen Publishing Group, Inc.
29 East 21st Street, New York, NY 10010

Author: John Hawkins
Editor and Picture Researcher: Joe Harris
U.S. Editor: Kara Murray
Design: Emma Randall
Cover Design: Emma Randall

Picture Credits:
B. Barber: 13. Corbis: cover, 1, 4, 8, 10, 12, 14, 15, 17, 19, 20, 21, 22, 26. Getty: 25. Mary Evans: 5, 6, 7, 9, 11, 16, 32. P. Gray: 18. Shutterstock: 23, 24, 27. T. Boyer: 28, 29.

Library of Congress Cataloging-in-Publication Data

Hawkins, John.
 Aliens and UFOs / by John Hawkins.
     p. cm. — (Mystery hunters)
 Includes index.
 ISBN 978-1-4488-6427-0 (library binding) — ISBN 978-1-4488-6437-9 (pbk.) — ISBN 978-1-4488-6438-6 (6-pack)
 1. Human-alien encounters—United States—Juvenile literature. 2. Unidentified flying objects—Sightings and encounters—United States—Juvenile literature. I. Title.
 BF2050.H375 2012
 001.942—dc23

                          2011019436

Printed in China
SL001925US

CPSIA Compliance Information: Batch #AW2102PK: For Further Information contact Rosen Publishing, New York, New York at 1-800-237-9932

CONTENTS

The UFOs Arrive 4

The "First" UFO 6

The Roswell Incident 8

The Mantell Incident 10

The Botta Encounter 12

The Kelly-Hopkinsville Encounter 14

The Interrupted Journey 16

The Socorro Incident 18

Incident at Valensole 20

The Exeter Incident 22

Man in Black 24

Fatal Encounter at Bass Strait 26

The Livingston UFO Assault...................... 28

Glossary.. 30

Further Reading, Web Sites 31

Index 32

THE UFOS ARRIVE

Public interest in UFOs, or unidentified flying objects, really began with the startling encounter reported by American pilot Kenneth Arnold in 1947. However, mysterious flying objects had been seen in the skies for many years before then. For example, cigar-shaped craft were seen over the United States in the 1890s, although these were probably early airships.

▲ Many UFOlogists believe that Earth has regularly been visited by aliens since the 1940s.

GHOST FLIERS

So-called ghost fliers were spotted on a number of occasions over Scandinavia between 1932 and 1937. In daylight they took the form of very large aircraft, much bigger than anything then flying. At night they shone dazzlingly bright searchlights onto the ground. According to eyewitness reports, they performed aerobatics and achieved speeds utterly impossible for any known aircraft.

FOO FIGHTERS

During World War II, strange glowing balls about 3 feet (1 m) across, known as foo fighters, were seen

A pair of foo fighters fly alongside a USAF B-24 Liberator bomber over Germany in 1944.

by both Allied and Axis pilots over Europe. They were observed flying alongside bomber formations for minutes at a time before either disappearing or flying off at high speed.

Pilots on both sides of the conflict assumed they were some form of enemy weapon and tried to shoot them down. But bullets appeared to have no effect on the crafts. What they actually were has never been discovered.

EXAMINING THE EVIDENCE

ARE UFOS REAL?

The witnesses whose stories have been told in this book were probably telling the truth, and believed they really did experience a visitation from another planet. But could their senses have been deceiving them? They might have misidentified astronomical objects such as clouds, planets, bright stars, meteors, artificial satellites, or the Moon. A number of UFO reports have been explained by flights of secret aircraft, weapons, and weather balloons or by light phenomena such as mirages and searchlights. Other UFO stories have turned out to be deliberate hoaxes. However, some UFO sightings have never been fully explained.

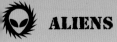

THE "FIRST" UFO

On the morning of June 24, 1947, Kenneth Arnold, an experienced American aviator, set off from Chehalis, Washington, to his home in Oregon in his single-engine Callier light aircraft. While flying over Mount Rainier, Arnold saw something that would change his life and usher in a new era.

▲ This artwork, signed by Kenneth Arnold, shows the aircraft he claimed to have seen. Arnold himself appears bottom left.

FLASH OF LIGHT

Arnold saw a bright flash of light sweep over his plane. Assuming this was caused by the sun reflecting off another nearby aircraft, Arnold hurriedly scanned the skies. Far to the north he saw a line of nine aircraft flying towards him at an angle.

As they came closer, Arnold realized that he was seeing something very strange indeed. Each aircraft was shaped like a wide crescent with neither fuselage nor tail. Moreover the aircraft were flying with a strange wavelike motion, quite unlike any known aircraft.

They dipped from side to side at times, the sun reflecting from their silver-blue surfaces. The formation was moving very fast. Arnold later estimated the speed at around 1,300 miles per hour (2,100 km/h), much faster than any known aircraft at that time.

FLYING SAUCERS

When he reached home, Arnold contacted a reporter, Bill Bacquette, at the *East Oregonian*, his local newspaper. Bacquette asked how the craft moved. Arnold said, "They flew like a saucer would if you skipped it across water." In his report, Bacquette referred to the craft as flying saucers. The term quickly became popular.

▲ Fate Magazine, *launched in 1948, led its first edition with the Arnold sighting.*

STRANGE STORIES
Two shadows
Arnold's experience prompted others to come forward with their own stories. A group of boys from Baradine, Australia, were rabbiting by moonlight one night in 1931. One boy noticed he was casting two shadows. Looking up he saw a disc-shaped object as bright as the Moon approaching from the northwest. Orange lights or flames flashed around its rim and the object rotated slowly as it flew. It followed a straight course before disappearing behind nearby hills.

THE ROSWELL INCIDENT

What really happened in early July 1947 at Roswell Air Force Base? On July 8, a press release from the base stated that a flying saucer had crashed near Roswell and the wreckage had been recovered. A few hours later, a second press release stated that the wreckage was actually from a weather balloon.

THE STORY IS REVIVED

Thirty years later, UFO researcher Stanton Friedman was put in touch with a former intelligence officer, Jesse Marcel, who served at Roswell. Marcel claimed he had been sent to the crash site to collect the debris and had never believed the weather balloon story. Friedman and his colleague William Moore tracked down other witnesses.

▼ This movie prop depicting an alien crash victim is on display at the International UFO Museum and Research Center, in Roswell.

▲ *In 1947, the US military released this image showing the wreckage from a weather balloon in response to press interest in the Roswell incident. But was this part of a cover-up?*

ALIEN BODIES?

In 1989, a mortician named Glenn Dennis claimed that the USAF medical team had called him in July 1947. He said they asked him detailed questions about how to preserve bodies. A USAF photographer then came forward to say he had seen and photographed four alien bodies at the base.

WITNESS INTERVIEWS

By 1980, they had interviewed 62 people. They came to believe something strange had happened at Roswell and that the United States Air Force (USAF) had covered it up. The witnesses claimed to have seen a UFO performing maneuvers impossible for any known aircraft. A rancher, W. "Mac" Brazel, had heard an explosion and found mysterious debris.

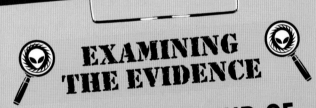

EXAMINING THE EVIDENCE

A DIFFERENT KIND OF COVER-UP?

Most of the evidence at Roswell was collected decades after the event, and not all of it was firsthand. An official USAF report has dismissed Friedman's claims. It admitted there had been a cover-up but this was because the crashed craft had been a top-secret Mogul high-altitude balloon, used for spying on the Soviets. However, many UFOlogists remain convinced that the USAF covered up something much more mysterious at Roswell.

THE MANTELL INCIDENT

At lunchtime on January 7, 1948, a UFO was spotted over Godman Air Force Base, in Kentucky. Colonel Guy Hix, commander at Godman, scrambled three P-51 fighter aircraft, which set off in pursuit of the mysterious object.

GIVING CHASE

Flight Commander Captain Thomas Mantell saw the object first as the three aircraft emerged from the clouds. The other two pilots radioed to say that they could see the object and Mantell's aircraft giving chase. But then clouds closed in again and they lost sight of the object and Mantell. Shortly afterwards, they returned to base. Mantell, meanwhile, was in hot pursuit. He sent three radio messages with updates on his progress, then nothing. After several minutes of radio

▲ Three fighter jets were scrambled to intercept the UFO over Kentucky.

▲ *This artist's impression captures the moment that Captain Mantell's P-51 Mustang fighter broke up in the air.*

over a large area of countryside. It had obviously broken up at high altitude and fallen to the ground in thousands of pieces. The P-51 was a famously robust fighter jet that did not fall to pieces for no reason.

silence from Mantell, Hix began to worry. More aircraft were scrambled to search the skies for the mysterious object and for Mantell's P-51, but they saw nothing.

FATAL CRASH

A few hours later the wreckage of Mantell's aircraft was found strewn

The death of Mantell turned the UFO phenomenon into an issue of deadly seriousness. It seemed unlikely that the USAF would allow its pilots to chase after one of their own secret weapons, and equally unlikely that the Soviet Union would risk testing secret aircraft in US airspace. So what did Mantell and his fellow pilots chase that day? We still have no idea.

EYEWITNESS TO MYSTERY
MANTELL'S FINAL RADIO MESSAGES
"The object is directly ahead of and above me now, moving at about half my speed. . . It looks metallic and it's tremendous in size." A few minutes later: . . . I'm still climbing. . . . I'm trying to close in for a better look." Last message: "It is still above me, making my speed or better. I'm going up to 20,000 feet (6,000 m). If I'm no closer then, I'll abandon the chase."

THE BOTTA ENCOUNTER

Dr. Enrique Botta was an engineer working on a building project in the rural area of Bahia Blanca in Venezuela. One evening in 1950, he was driving back to his hotel when he saw a strange object resting in a field. He stopped the car to take a look.

▼ Those who claim to have encountered aliens most often describe them as having bald, domed heads and large, black eyes.

INVESTIGATING THE OBJECT

According to Botta, the object was shaped like a domed disc made of a silvery metal. Its skin had a jellylike softness. There was an open door on one side. Botta walked through the door. He passed through a small, empty room into a second, larger room.

Here he saw three humanoid figures facing away from him. Each figure was about 4 feet (1.2 m) tall. Their heads were large and bald. They were facing a control panel filled with lights. Botta reached out and touched one of the figures. It was rigid. Believing the beings were dead, Botta fled back to his car.

▲ *In 1952, radio worker William Squyres encountered a UFO. Inside, he could see a pilot. This was one of the very earliest close encounters of the third kind.*

RETURN TO THE SITE

Botta told two of his colleagues at the hotel, and the three returned to the site the next morning. The craft had gone and all that remained was a pile of ashes. One of Botta's friends touched the pile and his hand turned purple. Botta meanwhile spotted a cigar-shaped UFO circling overhead. After a few minutes it flew away. Later that day, Botta collapsed with a fever and was rushed to hospital. He was diagnosed with severe sunburn.

FACT HUNTER

CLOSE ENCOUNTERS

What are they? Encounters with UFOs have been divided into three kinds:

- Close encounters of the first kind (CE1s)– sightings of UFOs
- Close encounters of the second kind (CE2s)– observation of UFOs and their physical effects, such as making crop circles
- Close encounters of the third kind (CE3s)– observation of aliens

When was the first CE3? The first reported CE3 took place in 1952 when radio worker William Squyres spotted a humanoid at the controls of a disc-shaped UFO hovering above a field in Kansas.

THE KELLY-HOPKINSVILLE ENCOUNTER

On August 21, 1955, Bill Taylor was visiting his neighbors, the Sutton family, at their remote farm between Kelly and Hopkinsville, Kentucky. At around 7 p.m., Taylor was getting water from the well when, he says, he saw a disc-shaped UFO floating down behind a line of trees.

▲ According to Bill Taylor, the aliens that attacked the Sutton family emerged from a UFO he had seen landing nearby.

STRANGE VISITOR

An hour later, Taylor and Elmer Sutton were in the kitchen when they saw a strange figure outside. They later claimed that it was around 3 feet (1 m) tall, walking upright on short legs with very long apelike arms. The creature had a large head, pointed ears, bulging eyes, and a slitlike mouth. It emitted a soft, silvery glow.

The being was joined by several more that began wandering around the farmyard. Sutton and Taylor picked up their guns and stepped out of the house. Sutton shouted a challenge. What did these creatures want?

▼ *After causing untold chaos, the aliens apparently slipped away into the woods.*

UNDER SIEGE

Taylor and Sutton returned to the house and heard footsteps on the roof. As Taylor stepped out, one of the aliens grabbed his hair in its long, spindly hands. Whipping around, he shot the alien. It flipped backwards over the roof, then fled into the darkness.

For the next three hours, the family remained, terrified, inside the house while the men took potshots at the aliens whenever they appeared. In the morning, they drove to the Hopkinsville police station and reported their story. The police found evidence of a battle at the farm but no aliens.

One of the aliens ran at them with arms held above its head. Sutton fired. The impact knocked the creature onto its back. After a moment, it got back to its feet and ran off, uninjured.

EYEWITNESS TO MYSTERY

"SOMETHING FRIGHTENED THESE PEOPLE"

Elmer Sutton was known in the area as a cool, tough farmer, not given to flights of fancy. The Suttons' story seemed outlandish, but the local police were inclined to take it seriously. Chief of Police Russell Greenwell later commented: "Something frightened these people. Something beyond their comprehension." Despite suffering ridicule, the Suttons and Taylor never changed their story. They remained convinced that they had come under attack that night and had been lucky to escape with their lives.

THE INTERRUPTED JOURNEY

At about 11 p.m. on September 19, 1961, Betty and Barney Hill were driving along Highway 3 near Lancaster, New Hampshire, when they saw a bright light in the sky. They pulled over to watch the object.

TIME DISCREPANCY

The object was oval shaped and bluish white. Through the row of windows on its front edge, humanoids could be seen moving around. Barney suddenly panicked. Convinced they were about to be attacked, he ushered his wife back in the car and then took off at high speed. They returned home at 5 a.m. and went straight to bed.

Five days later, Betty contacted UFOlogist Donald Keyhoe. Keyhoe pointed out that the encounter had

▲ *According to Betty and Barney Hill, they could remember being followed in their car by a UFO but not what happened next.*

lasted only a few minutes, yet they were two hours late getting home. Over the next few months, Betty and Barney suffered from nightmares and depression. They were sent to see Dr. Benjamin Simon who specialized in hypnotic regression.

▲ If aliens really do live among us, what are their plans for planet Earth?

TAKEN ABOARD

Under hypnosis, the Hills both said that their car was stopped by aliens standing in the road. They were taken to a landed UFO. Betty was forced to undergo painful medical experiments, then an alien showed her a map of the location of its home star system. The couple were taken back their car, after being told that they would not remember anything of the event.

? FACT HUNTER

ALIEN ABDUCTIONS

What are they? Alien abductions are seemingly real memories people have of being taken against their will by apparently nonhuman entities and subjected to physical and psychological tests.

When did they start happening? The first case to gain widespread attention was that of Antonio Villas Boas, a Brazilian farmer, who claimed to have been abducted by aliens in 1957.

Have there been many cases? There have been many hundreds of cases, particularly in the United States.

Do they really happen? Most scientists believe that alien abductions do not really happen but are a product of fantasy, false-memory syndrome, hallucination, hypnosis, and other psychological phenomena.

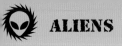
THE SOCORRO INCIDENT

On April 24, 1964, at around 5:45 p.m., Patrolman Lonnie Zamora was heading south from Socorro, New Mexico, in his police car in pursuit of a speeding motorist. He suddenly noticed a flash of bluish orange in the sky to the west followed by a roaring explosion. Fearing that the nearby dynamite shack had exploded, he gave up his chase to investigate.

▲ This artwork is based on Zamora's description of the craft and aliens.

TWO FIGURES

Zamora turned onto a rough gravel track. As he dipped into a shallow gully, the flame came again. It was shaped like a cone with the top narrower than the bottom. As he reached the top of the gully, Zamora saw an object with two figures standing beside it. The figures were wearing white overalls and may have had rounded caps or helmets.

THE OBJECT

When he looked again, the figures had vanished. Zamora got out of the car and approached the object, which was whitish silver and shaped like an from a safer distance to see the object hovering on its flame above the ground. Next time he looked, the flame and the roaring had stopped and the object hung eerily motionless. It then moved silently off towards the southwest before vanishing behind some hills.

▲ *UFO believers cite Patrolman Lonnie Zamora as a reliable witness because of his position of responsibility.*

oval standing on four legs. When Zamora was around 75 feet (23 m) from the object, a roaring began and a bluish-orange flame erupted from the base of the craft. Fearing for his life, Zamora turned and ran. He glanced back

EXAMINING THE EVIDENCE

ANALYZING THE TRACES

A prominent UFOlogist, Dr. Josef Hynek, was at the site two days later. He found burn marks on the ground where the craft had stood. Four deep rectangular marks were seen in the ground where heavy objects had pushed down into the dry soil. The marks were arranged as if on the circumference of a circle, as they would have been if there were four legs supporting a round object. Zamora was an excellent witness who was highly respected by his colleagues. Hynek concluded that a real, physical event of an unexplained nature had taken place.

INCIDENT AT VALENSOLE

Maurice Masse was a farmer in Valensole, France, one of the most rural parts of western Europe. He had no interest in UFOs and had never seen or read a science fiction movie or book. He had no obvious reason to invent a story. Yet here is what he claimed happened to him one July morning in 1965.

WHISTLING SOUND

Masse had stopped his tractor for a break when he heard a whistling sound coming from the other side of a small hill. He walked around the hill to investigate. He saw an egg-shaped, silver object mounted on six thin metal legs. Next to it were what he took to be two young boys with their backs to him, pulling at a lavender plant. Thinking they were vandals, he crept towards them.

PARALYZED

One of the "boys" turned around and whipped out a small gun-shaped object, which he pointed at Masse.

▲ *Masse's description of the "aliens" he encountered is remarkably consistent with the accounts of other witnesses.*

The farmer suddenly realized he was paralyzed. He could only look at the figures. They were about 4 feet (1.2 m) tall and had thin, slender bodies. Their heads were oval with pointy chins and large, slanting eyes. Their mouths were thin, lipless slits.

DEPARTURE

The figures made strange noises, but their mouths did not move. They floated up through an open hatch in the side of their craft, which rose vertically to around 60 feet (18 m), then flew away.

STRANGE STORIES
Similarities with Socorro

Some years after the incident at Valensole, a French UFO investigator sent Masse a drawing of the UFO that had landed at Socorro, New Mexico (see pages 18–19), as he thought it sounded similar. Masse's reaction was immediate and emphatic: "That is what I saw," he replied. "You see, I was not dreaming and I was not mad."

▲ The artist's impression of alien creatures is based on Maurice Masse's description.

THE EXETER INCIDENT

At 1 a.m. on September 3, 1965, Patrolman Eugene Bertrand was driving along Route 108 near Exeter, New Hampshire, when he saw a car parked by the side of the road. He pulled over and found a woman in some distress. She said her car had been followed by a bright white light in the sky that had hovered over the vehicle before flying off.

▲ Were the bright lights that Muscarello saw in fact alien spacecraft?

MUSCARELLO'S STORY

Bertrand returned to the Exeter police station at 2:30 a.m. There he found Norman Muscarello, who was shaking with fear. Eventually Bertrand got Muscarello's story out of him. Muscarello had been walking to Exeter along Route 150 when a group of five red lights came swooping down from the sky to hover over a house. The lights began to pulsate in a repetitive pattern before suddenly darting towards him, causing Muscarello to dive into a ditch. When he looked again, the lights were dropping beyond a line of trees, as if they were landing in the field beyond.

▼ *As they approached the UFO, Patrolman Bertrand drew his gun. However, he did not open fire.*

EXAMINING THE EVIDENCE

STICKING TO THEIR STORY

Bertrand and Hunt made a formal report about the Exeter incident. The Pentagon claimed the men must have mistaken a flight of B-47 military aircraft that had overpassed the area. Bertrand and Hunt pointed out they had spent many nights driving the highways and were familiar with B-47s. In any case, the B-47 flight had passed over around 1:30 a.m. and the sighting had continued until past 3 a.m. Later, the Pentagon agreed to reclassify the sighting as unidentified. The Exeter incident is interesting both because of the number of witnesses and because the police witnesses went to such lengths to defend their story.

SPOOKY LIGHTS

Bertrand drove Muscarello back to the field where he had seen the lights. They were about 50 feet (15 m) from the car when the cattle at a nearby farm began making alarmed noises. Suddenly the red lights rose up from the ground behind the trees. Bertrand drew his pistol as the lights came closer but did not fire. The two men hid behind the car as the lights approached to within 100 feet (30 m). Bertrand radioed for backup. By the time Patrolman David Hunt arrived, the red lights had retreated to about 1/3 mile (.5 km) away. They rose into the sky and headed rapidly away.

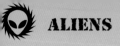

MAN IN BLACK

In 1976, Dr. Herbert Hopkins, a doctor and hypnotist, was regularly meeting UFO witness David Stephens to discuss his experience. Hopkins claims that he received a phone call on the evening of September 11 from a man claiming to be vice president of the New Jersey UFO Research Organization. The man asked if he could drop by to discuss the Stephens case. Hopkins agreed.

▲ Was the man in black who visited Herbert Hopkins human or something more sinister?

STRANGE VISITOR

According to Hopkins, the man arrived at his home just moments later. He was dressed in a black suit with sharply creased pants, black hat, black shoes, black tie, gray gloves and white shirt. Hopkins invited the man in and asked him to sit down. The man removed his hat to reveal that he was totally bald. His head and face were pale. The two men chatted for a while about the Stephens case. Hopkins noticed that his guest spoke in a curiously flat, emotionless monotone. Even stranger, he was wearing lipstick that came off on his glove when he brushed his lips with his fingers.

DISAPPEARING TRICK

Suddenly, the man asked Hopkins for a coin. Hopkins says he handed one over and was surprised to see it vanish from the man's open palm. The man then explained he could make a heart vanish from within a human body just as easily. He ordered Hopkins to stop working on the Stephens case and to destroy all his files. By now thoroughly terrified, Hopkins agreed.

The man then began to slur his words. He stood abruptly and said, "My energy is running low and I must go now." The man walked with some difficulty out of the house.

Outside, Hopkins saw a bright bluish light that he took to be car headlights. Later, Hopkins found odd marks on his driveway unlike those that would have been left by a car. He discovered there was no such thing as the New Jersey UFO Research Organization. He dropped the Stephens case and destroyed the files.

▲ According to Hopkins, the mysterious man made a coin vanish into his hand.

? FACT HUNTER

MEN IN BLACK

Who are they? "Men in black" are men dressed in black suits who claim to be officials of secret organizations or government agents. They threaten UFO witnesses to keep quiet about what they have seen.

How do they behave? They usually have detailed information on the people they contact. They are often confused by everyday items such as pens or eating utensils.

Who are they really? Some UFOlogists believe men in black are in fact aliens or androids controlled by aliens sent out to cover up alien activity on Earth. Others think they are government agents seeking to hush up UFO sightings. A third theory is that they are hallucinations caused by the trauma of encountering a UFO.

FATAL ENCOUNTER AT BASS STRAIT

On the evening of October 21, 1978, 20-year-old pilot Frederick Valentich was flying from Melbourne, Australia, to King Island. He took off in his Cessna 182 at 6:19 p.m. and by 7 p.m. he was flying over Bass Strait, the stretch of sea between Tasmania and mainland Australia.

NEAR MISS

At 7:06 p.m. Valentich radioed Melbourne Flight Control to ask if there were any other aircraft in his area. Melbourne replied that no known aircraft were around. There was a slight pause, then Valentich reported that a large aircraft showing four bright lights had just flown by 1,000 feet (300 m) above him.

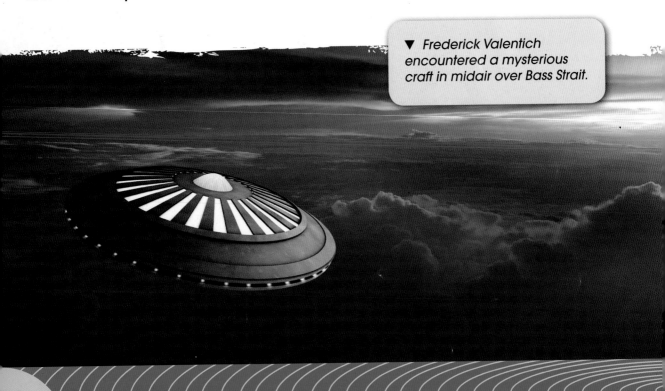

▼ Frederick Valentich encountered a mysterious craft in midair over Bass Strait.

"IT'S NOT AN AIRCRAFT"

At 7:09 p.m. Valentich reported, "It seems to be playing some sort of game with me." Melbourne asked if he could identify the aircraft. "It's not an aircraft," came the surprising response. "It is flying past. It has a long shape." There was a pause, then he cried, "It's coming for me right now." Then Valentich seemed to calm down. "I'm orbiting and the thing is orbiting on top of me. It has a green light and a sort of metallic light on the outside."

VANISHED

All seemed well until 7:12 when Valentich came back on the radio to say, "Engine is rough and coughing… Unknown aircraft is on top of me." There was a burst of static, then silence. Melbourne repeatedly tried contacting Valentich but received no response. At 7:28 p.m., Melbourne ordered a search to begin. No sign of Valentich or his Cessna was ever found.

▼ The lighthouse at Cape Otway, Victoria, overlooking the wild southern seas over which Frederick Valentich's aircraft vanished.

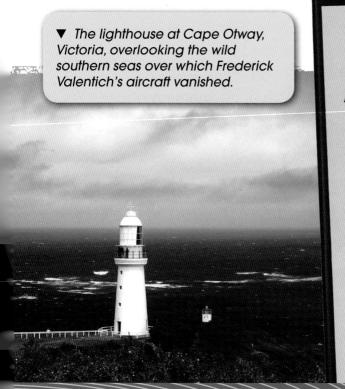

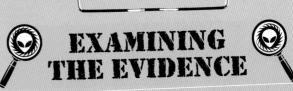

EXAMINING THE EVIDENCE

FLYING UPSIDE DOWN?

Over the weeks following Valentich's disappearance there were many attempts to explain what happened. One suggestion was that Valentich had somehow turned the aircraft upside down and was seeing the reflection of his own lights in the sea. However, he had the UFO in sight for about 7 minutes and the Cessna can fly upside down for only 30 seconds before the fuel system collapses.

THE LIVINGSTON UFO ASSAULT

▼ Taylor claimed that he was attacked by two black spheres with spiked legs.

At 10 a.m. on November 9, 1979, Scottish forestry worker Robert Taylor walked into a forest outside Livingston, Scotland, west of Edinburgh. In a clearing in the forest he encountered a dark gray, hovering object about 20 feet (6 m) across. It was round with a thin rim around its base.

BLACK SPHERES

According to Taylor's account, he stopped in alarm. Almost at once he saw he was being approached by two black balls coming from the direction of the object. Each one was a little under 3 feet (1 m) in diameter and had six legs on its surface. The balls rolled towards him on their legs, making soft sucking noises as each leg touched the ground. Before he could retreat, a leg from each sphere grabbed hold of his leg with another soft sucking sound. The balls began dragging Taylor back towards the object. Taylor struggled to free himself. There was now a burning stench so intense he could barely breathe. He felt himself growing dizzy and losing consciousness.

▼ *Robert Taylor's account of his encounter with extraterrestrial life raises the worrying possibility that aliens could have hostile feelings towards us.*

EXAMINING THE EVIDENCE

MARKS IN THE SOIL

The police went to the clearing and examined marks in the soil. They found two parallel tracks, 8 feet (2.5 m) long and 1 foot (30 cm) wide. These were formed from crushed grass as if a very heavy weight had rested on them. Around these tracks were two circles of holes driven into the soil. Each hole was circular, about 4 inches (10 cm) across and 6 inches (15 cm) deep. There were 40 holes in all, driven in at an angle away from the tracks. No heavy machinery had been used in the clearing for months. The police found the marks to be consistent with Taylor's story.

INJURED

He woke up 20 minutes later, lying face down on the grass. The strange objects had all gone. Taylor's pants were torn where the objects had grabbed him. One of his legs was badly bruised and his chin was cut and bleeding. He couldn't stand and had to crawl back to his truck. When he got home, he called his boss and told him his story.

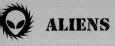
GLOSSARY

abductions (ab-DUK-shunz) Forcibly taking people away against their will.

aerobatics (er-uh-BA-tiks) Feats of spectacular flying.

airship (ER-ship) A lighter-than-air, power-driven aircraft kept buoyant by a body of gas.

circumference (ser-KUMP-fernts) The enclosing boundary of a curved shape, especially a circle.

debris (duh-BREE) Scattered fragments of something wrecked or destroyed.

diameter (dy-A-meh-ter) A straight line passing from side to side through the center of a shape, especially a circle or sphere.

discrepancy (dis-KREH-pun-see) A lack of compatibility or similarity between two or more facts.

false-memory syndrome (FAWLS-mem-ree SIN-drohm) A condition in which a person's identity and relationships are affected by memories that are factually incorrect but strongly believed.

fuselage (FYOO-seh-lahzh) The main body of an aircraft.

gully (GUH-lee) A water-worn ravine.

hallucination (huh-loo-suh-NAY-shun) An experience involving the apparent perception of something not present.

humanoid (HYOO-muh-noyd) Having an appearance resembling that of a human.

hypnosis (hip-NOH-sus) The induction of a state of consciousness in which a person apparently loses the power of voluntary action and is highly responsive to suggestion or direction.

hypnotic regression (hip-NO-tik rih-GREH-shun) A process of taking a person back to an earlier stage of life through hypnosis.

maneuvers (muh-NOO-verz) Movements requiring skill and care.

meteors (MEE-tee-orz) Small bodies of matter from outer space that enter the Earth's atmosphere and appear as streaks of light.

mirage (muh-RAHZH) An optical illusion caused by atmospheric conditions.

monotone (MO-nuh-tohn) A voice that is unchanging in pitch and without intonation.

mortician (mawr-TIH-shun) A person whose business is preparing dead bodies for burial or cremation.

paralyzed (PER-uh-lyzd) Partly or wholly incapable of movement.

phenomena (fih-NO-meh-nuh) Facts or situations that are observed to exist or happen.

psychological (sy-kuh-LO-jih-kul) Of, affecting, or arising in the mind; related to the mental and emotional state of a person.

pulsate (PUL-sayt) A regular, rhythmic brightening and dimming.

scrambled (SKRAM-buld) Ordered (a fighter aircraft) to take off immediately in an emergency.

spindly (SPIND-lee) Long and thin.

star system (STAHR SIS-tem) A large number of stars with a perceptible structure; a galaxy.

trauma (TRAW-muh) A deeply distressing or disturbing experience.

UFOlogists (yoo-FO-luh-jists) People who study UFOs.

weather balloon (WEH-ther buh-LOON) A balloon with special equipment that is sent into the atmosphere to provide information about the weather.

FURTHER READING

Davis, Barbara J. *The Kids' Guide to Aliens*. Mankato, MN: Capstone, 2009.

Evans, Christopher. *Aliens and UFOs*. London: Carlton Books, 2009.

Grace, N. B. *UFOs: What Scientists Say May Shock You!* Danbury, CT: Children's Press, 2008.

Oxlade, Chris. *The Mystery of UFOs*. Can Science Solve?. Mankato, MN: Heinemann Library, 2007.

WEB SITES

Due to the changing nature of Internet links, PowerKids Press has developed an online list of Web sites related to the subject of this book. This site is updated regularly. Please use this link to access the list:

www.powerkidslinks.com/mysthunt/aliens/

INDEX

abduction 17
aircraft 4, 5, 6, 7, 9, 10, 11, 23, 26, 27
aliens 4, 8, 9, 12, 13, 14, 15, 17, 18, 20, 21, 22, 25, 29
Arnold, Kenneth 4, 6, 7

balls 4, 28
Bertrand, Eugene 22, 23
Botta, Enrique 12–13

car 12, 16, 17, 18, 22, 23, 25
close encounters 13
crash 8, 11

encounter 4, 12, 13, 16, 26, 29
evidence 5, 9, 15, 19, 23, 27, 29
Exeter, New Hampshire 22
experiments 17
extraterrestrial life 29

flying saucer 7, 8
foo fighters 4
Friedman, Stanton 8

ghost fliers 4
Godman Air Force Base 10

hallucination 17, 25
Hill, Betty and Barney 16, 17
Hopkins, Herbert 24, 25
humanoid 13, 16
Hynek, Josef 19
hypnosis 17
hypnotic regression 16

lights 6, 7, 12, 16, 22, 23, 25, 26, 27

Mantell, Thomas 10–11
Marcel, Jesse 8
Masse, Maurice 20, 21
men in black 25
mirage 5
Muscarello, Norman 22, 23

pilot 4, 5, 10, 11, 13, 26
police 15, 29

Roswell Air Force Base 8

scientists 17
Socorro, New Mexico 18–19, 21
sounds 20, 28
spacecraft 22
Stephens, David 24
Sutton, Elmer 14, 15

Taylor, Bill 14, 15
Taylor, Robert 28
tracks 18, 29

UFOlogist 4, 9, 16, 19, 25
UFOs 4, 5, 6, 9, 10, 13, 14, 16, 17, 19, 20, 21, 23, 25, 27
United States Air Force (USAF) 9, 11

Valensole, France 20–21
Valentich, Frederick 26–27

weather balloon 5, 8, 9

Zamora, Lonnie 18, 19